ELEMENOPY

Michael Coffey

Elemenopy

NEW AMERICAN POETRY
SERIES: 22

SUN & MOON PRESS
LOS ANGELES • 1996

Sun & Moon Press
A Program of The Contemporary Arts Educational Project, Inc.
a nonprofit corporation
6026 Wilshire Boulevard, Los Angeles, California 90036

This edition first published in paperback in 1996 by Sun & Moon Press
10 9 8 7 6 5 4 3 2 1
FIRST EDITION
©1996 by Michael Coffey
Biographical material ©1996 by Sun & Moon Press

This book was made possible, in part, through an operational grant from
the Andrew W. Mellon Foundation, through a matching grant from
the National Endowment for the Arts, and through contributions to
The Contemporary Arts Educational Project, Inc.,
a nonprofit corporation

Cover: Auguste Herbin, *Vitaliste,* 1959
Design: Katie Messborn
Typography: Guy Bennett

LIBRARY OF CONGRESS CATALOGING IN PUBLICATION DATA
Coffey, Michael. [1954]
Elemenopy / Michael Coffey
p. cm — (New American Poetry Series: 22)
ISBN: 1-55713-240-2
I. Title. II. Series: New American Poetry Series; NAP 22.
PS3553.O362E44 1995
811'.54—dc20
95-26122
CIP

Printed in the United States of America on acid-free paper.

Contents

Loving

Love Poetry

Let's talk and we do
talk. A page is torn.
Pull up and steer deep
chairs and things and sit.
We talk and we do
talk.

A frame is formed.
Rooms of infinite
patience. The lights off.
Cares and things are set.
Let's fuck and we do
fuck.

Children aren't born.
Rooms are infinite
spaces, and nights are.
Fears and things unspent
take walks. And we do
walk.

Old parallels
run on down the line.
Fiving, fiving, five
in a kind of 'v'
that meets out there, un-
seen.

So is it a her
I ask and she says
it's a she. I say
I'm sure it's a book
I miss, a book I
miss.

Regular mar-
gins? They're common, Tess.
I like that name here.
I'm committed, thanks,
to six-line stanzas,
the

last line one word.
A frame of a sort,
the beat of a minute.
I'm committed, thanks,
to sex with stanzas,
love,

and you're in it.

Predation

Taut princess
of the neighborhood
caught on a vine
and unwinding the

blue confines
and the red or some say
"read" that's too

self-conscious to be wrong
or is it self-aware I mean to
say, or meant to, that

then unwinds
this caught princess
of the neighborhood.

Round

Walls falling all around
through histories and towns.
Never a wall built
that won't come down.
So why go on about it?

Rounded surfaces, the rolling globe
smooth as a baby's cheek,
not a blemish upon it, nothing
fallen or to fall.

Perfect sphericity
as in the sound of purr
and the curve of down
on thee.

Lawrentian

Assonance at every instance, or every other.
Offal odor, effable—the less for it—
leaving autumn eager and overrun.

Oblation, time of need; gourd-like
and engorging. Pearls, purses full,
gulp up awesome dishes of a sound.

Of a fissioning and the pound of it
burst finally, plum-bruised and stewing,
the low sun brown with bees.

Hortense

Hortense: the aphid enclosures of a lust bloom. Soporific. Just and menial, menses muddies all. To be swept in cane sugar, wrested away. That is a slap at luxury.

Tawny to a point. An old curmudgeon lunches long. Plays out the slipper game and stays late. Action peaks, powder and words. Ablest is armature to fame.

A fast track, you bet. The slow, tough, technical terms of youth. Such as sentiment, obelisk, herd. All but a seamlessness and touch football. Makes for the overs and the unders.

Top it off. Add the elocution, or starve. Either send it out or seethe. Hate is always in even the loveliest mail. A pint o' bitter, lad. And sir. Brave the matron's way—

But hold it!
—carries too much up there, with slap and essay.
So with this.

The overblown objects. Optical rights obtunded. Oh that there were such rights.

Optimal, as in the main mind. Up there, indeed-o, with map and play.

Loveable. Otis. And charmed.

Opticianist—with a dull glare. Even as a level: amber, gellid eyes.

Oddnesses again, those o's again. We are open. Optimistic.

Put them away like objects put away to be saved. Not exactly the smaller the better—need constitution. Objects that are put away are owned and seen over; they don't become free. Overseen cum owned.

Thing

Thing is made of six words.

The third word will be the last word.

And the next to fourth word is next to next to last.

Next, the word next to to.

Inkling

Inkling linkages, the active verb.
Iamb inkling linkages
of a fist thud and seniority
the "one" must feel the linkages of
in a chain.

Or the rhyme—
sedimentation of a line
within or exempted, aligned
or renown, children in,
Paris-bound. Irruption.

So what is it today?
Dorchester…or such sounds.
Or is it me?
Does anybody know?
Is it simply this: that limitation
is again to be charmed?

Planting It

planting it stamping it stomping it
stopping it. painting it, planking down.
planing it taming it. taking down.
blanking it. ground out, rout.

Plains. The flat affluvial fix of Nairobi.
Eastern wick, wind under kinship, pound
in a dust heap—
a sheep shit townhouse tumble—
some warble, blur...
  Cows, inken owls, the wiles
in sunlit white, lost from view. The few
last rights. Howls of juveniles simply put:
words in a lost tongue, dead
first son of a brother's ex-wife,
jars of flies making going do.

Isinglass

...The indexation of isinglass is I *sing,* not *is* sing, is a
slithering hard sometimes.
Is a consciousness of.
?
Of a bleat out and some blowing. The wind thing...
Breath in water, air.
Of a following like
or seeming clearly like. Surface up
and glissando.

Clear. Small and smooth.
As reference to itself is. The air
of bladder water holds.

Cold hail, glass matter.
Knife and fucking fish.

Oslo

So one shouts it
lords around it with a round mouth.
Gobs gobble, the oaf, oafish, opens.
Woe is wood more oval than owed.

Action asks it, natch.
Face force close on it
like a bead
a bit like, a bit like

a small screw in a screen.

Say that utter image—
a bullet in the teeth
sleeves rolled
reel in the victual.

Clean as biscuits
white as snow
cold as ocean foam.

A Beer Is a Boat with a Crew

Moving things out and away.
Down.
Moving things out with the hands.
Evening out
to a paste, then,
then thinning it out, like sand.
Leveling the forms out. Leveling out
out.

Evening, not as night time
but as a fall towards a mean.
Even in this.
Even if not.
Even if
the endlessly, gently probing doors.
Even if the fallacy.
Even if talking
one talks
about the self.
Even if one does.

Image is a limp word
of slight rapid sounds.
Sounds like *accomplishment*: many
m's and consonants, a chew too.
Bounty, weal. Olive branch.

Image
is a limp word. And what
about the sound—
bees in a glass, the light
froth in formula. Milk
weeds of imagery
of a sounding
of a making sound.

As in Over

Oceans are the hands, oceans are the fast hands.
Oceans are the hands, oceans are the hands
over oceans, like an ocean wave wave waving.
Oceans are the hands. Fast ocean hands.

Running fast ocean hands over hands. Waves…
Hands waving over ocean hands over ocean hands over hands.
Oceans are the hands if the fast hands.
Fast ocean hands waving ocean hands waving.

Oceans are the hands, oceans are the fast hands.
Oceans hands waving ocean hands always waving.
Hands. Ocean. Hands. Ocean. Waves. Waving. Hands.
Oceans. Waves nip. The surface. A million lips.

Planking

A planking of white sentence, bald as a novitiate at the keys: like a platform not yet built; butterflies flitting in a lumberyard.

A raft is what he's after: loll fit shifting. A swell is a long wave that moves continuously like a sine, jetsam gellid on the sea.

Something sunken grinds the hull.

Passengers in passing less articulate than grief, the sound of lumber lowly rubbed, rubbing. In a hold, fresh cut and not too old, numbers on the edges, four the edge.

The room ripples. Sleeper swimming back, arming up, this crawl, coming. Army up, appalled. Humming: she is known.

Bed clothes don't rustle, they move. Sure is a damning, the pert is fooled. Bedimming. Then again the limbing, as in loving.

Light in a stammer.

"Electric switch" is nearly right for the act of execution. A face flames in a mirror most mornings and moves closer.

She has a tiny pencil. She licks its tip. She underlines each eye.

A Fact of Language

Despair
is raped. Dies. Spars idea.

Sides rap. Raps. Pair a dice.
Sad rips, sea. Seas rip, rap.
Rap dies.

Rap said: ear, as paid.
Dip air.

Rid apes, sir. Ride.
Air sped, a spider. Air raid.
Peas, seas, sad as pies. A pier.

Dire, asp. A rise rises.
Drips repaid, a spread, said:

Red, a air. Spare
sped as id, aspire.
Said per and dire.

Aspired, as ride is.
As pride is.
Is praised.

The News

Round oval pounds.
Loose lips on a lollipop.
Organ donors and gorgeous days:
slay of whip.

Tanqueray (Yea!). Bottle of soap.
Odious rumors run free.
Ballroom poster, floor.
Trashing cashing flow.

Pontificate. Certificate. Arithmetic.
For sure.
Items aging accident:
exceedingly grave.

Dropster punster opens aisles.
Draft after show-talk biz
takes the day.

Caption: Astor on a street.
Doesn't glib easily, the flip.

Obtuse the angle heat,
fair the tree.

Resolution

Old brown dreams.
If it may be for me.
If it may be.
If it may be for me.
I'll get it.

Stay
with a brown bag.
Stand with one
in your goddamn hand.
Let me talk to you.

With a brown bag
to carry it in
and throw it out.
I'll talk to you.

Stones

Cold narration
ice water over ice
clarity cleansing glass
and cooling passion.

Odds are it's a woman
or things to do with money.
If it's both the joints are chilled
beyond moving.

Not to warm it,
that's the key:
keep the breath of bravery,
strongly watch things die.

February and water flow
fast as breathless air;
anxious getting and anxious there:
what is left are simple stones.

Lichen

Marie

Marie's left foot just slipped. Jim was there. Just slipped and fell. On the ice on the walk. To Mass. Head hit the ice in no sound. All kneeled, they said.

That was that was it. Roomy eyes after. Jim was good. Jim was there. Jim was always wise.

Marie, they said Marie. Book in bed and read what? Drainage whispers. Brain drainage winter night and fall. Go to Boston Brooklyn Bridge, long tall to weather where was ought to.

Cold as. As slab on ice. Hours thank my back. Think Marie. Coldest steel is ice. Bought my back, back is what his ice is. Stop truck doing. Hair stuck it did and eyes cold.

Jim was there. Hands. Knees and air in days itch a wooly way like air does itch, always. Thanks a lot. A phone's a bank. Super.

Openers for years had passed. A switch swished back of a tail. Gonest is the wind. Mind it, he said. The things to be had about the way.

Barb was a beaut, my little one. Barb was big now up

and lovely. And Jim, Jim was there. Lovely and her lips a little one.

Back he said, and often. Back to way. I was washing, washing days. Eating, always eat. Eat a strong gas heat, ring come rise up pop and blue. Eat always, gas the clothes.

Marbles, she wants marbles. How they rang a cup and carpet rolls. Skid on kids one of 'em. Left foot slips and the back a purple, new ways. Single thing froze, days, oh days, a clear. Blue lines or she'd geometry. Passed.

Said me up. Ah, ma chair. Chair, chair, chair picked at. Don't pick but picked on holes in arms and finger warms. Laid there did always in clothes.

Taken out, care of me. Take care of me. All rise.

What is it. One is it. Who is it? Jim? Talk is it, can. Wet is it. Double you double you Jim, he said. What if it isn't?

Backed up now for fears. Jim was there but her. Her there not Jim, my Barb, my little one. A her. Her Jim. Jim was there. Jim, Jim, Jim.

Jim was there, moved. Fluttered, a bird. No carpets, and cold I'll bet. Dear Paul. Paulie is a friend of yours. Paulie a friend. Out of out. Paulie is a lout. Paulie is a friend of yours. Or out.

Setting on the ya, a bone. It's dry. Setting on it over there. Heat warms hands. Not the light much. Anymore. Not the light.

Dark made the curtains bright. And pull. Paul says he don't say much. Paulie stays up drunk. Sits and stays and says. Take care of me?

Nights like over, over, over. Under curtains bright curtains move. Under light, street. Car car chill. No one up, no down. Barb, miss my little one.

And Jim was there. Just slipped, slipped. Fell to way. Life like that all rolled. Donuts up, chew yes. Paulie has his, does his own, his shirts. Burned maybe. All rise in burn maybe. But Jim is there, so sweet. Sweet is Jim. Is her. Barb should buy, buy fast. Not Paulie, his shirts. Paulie is a friend of yours. Paulie hand your shirt.

Rubber runs the lotion, Doctor says. Judge says O my god. No oh. Blame a tree, a walk. Rain came the next day, undone is done. Paulie stays. Says a day, a ship, made him Jim. A slip? Jim for days, out of work a week. Spell away, go away. Go broke. Where is the Barb, a little one? My little one? Jim, no Jim, Jim. A her. Her, her, her. Marie. Want Marie.

Domingo

I

He was always after talent. His tongue turned at the mention of speed, where he could see only dust and victory; at the promise of power and precision, which gave one the upper hand in the wrestle with event. His teams had torn the league for years; his people had produced. Hell—he started chewing cigars.

His wife was dead and so were his children. She'd had an accident with a gardening tool—insane! And the boys had been lost in a bus crash in a bayou. So now he was traveling alone with all the necessary maps, looking for Latins with live bats. Ole!

As far as he could he was traveling by car, a bubble of his extended consciousness, a space he could control. His blues, his smokes, his hair oil. South to the Keys and then a boat; then a rented car on the island, looking for Domingo.

Domingo—nearly white, they say. Tall for a Dominican and hard as oak. It was said he'd bat with his forearm

as a joke, and crush the ball without flinching: he had a
knob on his arm like a ball.

What's to be said about ways? Tan slacks angle under
the "O" of the steering wheel and fall down toward
cuffs and slender loafers over thin tan socks. His feet
deftly shift gears, clutch up then a tassel flap and a light
release of the gas. Inside, the car just hums its hundred
sounds.

I've got to get this guy from New York to Florida. I
don't know the way.

Perhaps he just arrives. He encounters the need for a
parking space in a convenient garage. He fulfills the need
on the twelfth level of a concrete spiral, lodged in a dark
cell between two motionless, empty cars.

From interior to interior, not really of a different kind.
I could have him take his slacks off, or don a swimming
shell. I could hold him captive to the self.

He takes his bags. Why not a hotel room? Or a bar?
The challenge is temperance. He decides against it.

Elevator takes him down the twelve levels. The day
strikes him as yellow and warm and unpleasant.

His question is simple: The hotel bar? The answer: "The
Green Door," and indeed it was. The place was plush

with green and wood and brass planters. Scotch was in order. A double.

Ah... another interior. Perfect. And another? Perhaps I'll take my man to the toilet, rough him up a bit. Get him drunk or shot or killed or raped or gored or robbed simply, or caught in a bomb attack or scalded by a burst pipe. A movement large enough to hide inside of...

II

Conversation happened. A man laid a rolled newspaper across his arm, pointed it toward his face like a mike and said, I wanna show you something, and proceeded to shoot himself in the foot. The first thing our man Moses noticed—for that was his name—was the jump of sawdust followed by the stun of report and one amazed look on the face of the man with the newspaper, his eyes instantly wet and his mouth as if it had just taken a punch, wobbly open and limp. He'd pulled the trigger digging in his coat pocket.

He turned to walk out and left Moses the newspaper. He actually said to him, "Here," as if it were a gift. The rims of his ears were red. He did not stagger, but walked perfectly straight until the last two steps through the door, which he took in a skip, favoring his right foot. The bright daylight through the door hung on Moses's retina like a sheet drifting on a line.

Moses could see the man for a moment, hobbled over, raising his hand to hail a cab.

The young bartender leapt from behind the bar with a knife and bent down beneath Moses to dig the bullet out. He dug, and gouged, swore a bit in Spanish; he finally asked Moses to move. "Señor, please." Finally successful, he presented the find like a kid playing dentist and dropped it in a shot glass. It looked like a very bad tooth.

The scotch has its wonderful snap—it has a back palate attack like no other liquor. Man Moses meditates upon the distinctions in distilled spirits: whiskey, smooth but barky unless Canadian, then frothy with sweet; tequila, the taste of fermented flesh; vodka, base and aromatic like methyl; gin suggestive of some aftershave.

We have to get him out of here.

Moses arrives in Latin America. A noble sentence. He's got a bag full of bats, brand new Tennessee ash. An American on the make? Moses wouldn't argue.

First of all, Domingo. Domingo lives in Domingo, and Domingo, first of all, is full of flies. Not horseflies—you don't get those winged raisins as up north. You see big raspberries with green wings and dark stone-like objects with a blur of white wing action. They can fall across your face as a shadow, momentarily blocking the sun, a dish rag you try to elude, and you do. They go. They don't bite, just hover and dive a bit.

There are aluminum cans all over the town of Domingo. There's a large bin in the center of town where the government collects cans as a form of taxation. There's an election of sorts coming up.

Domingo sits on the back patio of a downtown restaurant. He looks like a piece of lawn furniture—dressed in white, his skin brown as the other browns in the yard: bark and old adobe.

Domingo has hit a hundred home runs the last two years, playing nearly two hundred games a year. He's said to be unnervingly quick. Despite his size he plays short. His right arm is like a taut fire hose, once-knotted at the elbow where muscle and tendon leap across the joint.

Our man Moses is here for a reason. A quick deal would cut his work to a nice trim; perhaps he could get some sun. Domingo was the one.

Domingo speaks excellent English. He has quit smoking. To busy his hands he is constantly drawing, scribbling and shading stick figures on a pad, regularly tearing a sheet off to start another. He is twenty-nine.

So he isn't a long-range prospect any more. No one in years has seen him as a "prospect"; but he is known goods and thought capable of producing at the major league level, almost immediately. But as always, just as much today as ten years ago, he wants too much money.

When he was a lesser player, when he was not yet twenty and didn't switch hit, back when he had "promise," he wanted an outrageous 200 grand. It was anybody's guess what he wanted now. No one had asked him in some time. But Moses has a guess, and a plan.

This is it. Moses figures Domingo will want 600 grand from a big club; there is no question in Moses's mind that Domingo would play every day, once he makes it; but no club will stake that kind of cash on a 29-year-old who has never played a game north of Havana, certainly not on Moses's word, who, despite a good reputation, had once sung the virtues of a bonus baby who bombed. And they never let him forget it. But Moses is willing to gamble that Domingo can command good money—better than the 600 grand—once he proves himself, as Moses knows he will.

The deal would be this: Moses proposes a "secret" deal to pay Domingo 400 grand out of his own pocket (he is selling his house in Westchester, now that his wife is gone), and sign him to a big club for 200. No problem. Domingo gets his 600 g's for the year, minus Moses's commission on the ball club contract. But in the contract, Moses ties an extension to Domingo's performance in the first year—two more years for 2.2 million if Domingo plays in 135 games, and hits .300 and drives in more than 80 runs. In a separate agreement with Domingo, Domingo agrees to pay Moses a 50% commission on the total package of the extension. So, when all is said and done, Domingo gets $1.7 mill for three years and Moses turns his $400,000 investment into a million one.

III

Domingo doesn't drink. He is a role model for his countrymen. His father had been a poet. His verses are still chanted at gatherings of the revolutionary left.

Domingo sits, scribbling intensely but at a great remove from the pad due to the stretch of his long brown arm. Moses loves this arm as he steps out to the patio from the dark front bar. In slow motion he sees this arm nail a quick succession of runners at first base with throws that seem headed for the ground upon leaving the hand but which rise into the first baseman's mitt knee-high with tremendous pop.

They trade pleasantries, but Domingo draws it to a close. "Dinero," he says, "has dinner in it. We must eat, no?" His laugh rattles like small wooden blocks falling on the table and scattering across it to fall in a second of silence to the laid stones below where they chatter to a stop. His grin is broad and white. "My people need money. I will play for them."

Moses explains his view that Domingo's people cannot be helped by him. "They will do nothing for me," says Moses. "I am not interested in them, Domingo. I am interested in you. I can help you."

Domingo reaches into the pocket of his white trousers and pulls out a gun. He shoots Moses in the forehead. Laughter fills the back patio like excited birds. Domingo begins to draw a picture of a man.

Otherwards

Sweet Suite: Gertrude Stein

1. POETRY AND GRAMMAR

Lively and the same words written
about.
Not as lively words as the words
grammar and with poetry
use nouns.
Are a lot of other things besides nouns.
Grammar grammar is
ever been, more.

And incidentally one's self.
Sentences of course.

Adjectives are not
really interesting.
Equally true of its adverb.
Adjectives never can
look like themselves.

That is the reason
he talked about a rose.
I hope now no one
need not make any one
go with them.

Nouns which have been names
one might have in one's list
there. So much for that.

Are some punctuations
not. Of these, the.

Is the question
mark.
It is evident
therefore. I ask you therefore.
And so it pleases
that a question
I never could bring
or the printing
now anybody sees.

Obvious and so
felt that way.

See and I do see.
One does do.
Unnecessary and not

now to come.
Do feel that.
Semicolons to do with it what.

Come back to how of Americans.
Look at it and in.
Of their very very
right, being in.
So then in.

Inevitably, no matter.
Not really
them.
Express itself.
Life of their own they are.
Lively they are or disguised.
Excessive complications, would you want
comma as I did.
Think about anything
upon you. Make you
a period. Does
little different but more so and later.

Really do.
Exist and have a vocabulary.
Combine by making enormously long.
Read anything in order.
Expected them to be.
And what said I, when a train,

the connection that
I said of Henry James
once. I think I did.
Never had before has sighed.

Nearly ready they had ordered it to close
out essentially what prose is.

Do as anybody does.
One and one and
up of sentences.
But, and after,
try to tell a little.

As you all know.
Be avoided, what takes place.
Other things with short and long.
Unemotional balance.
That is what prose is and that.

In prose of course.
That by thinking of.
Less difficult to know
of which
noun as prose is.
Good deal. Anybody or anything lives.

And feelings
still too.

Happening could be made.
Until now and always.
May be repeated in.
Are the names.
Now the poetry has changed.
Is the same.
Think what you do when you do.
You do.

2. PORTRAITS AND REPETITION

Nothing
makes nothing
makes any difference
if the
same
person talking
and the listening
does the talking and the listening.

And the listening.
Doing both
as if they were
like the motor going
inside the car
and the car moving
part of the same thing.

It were possible
of this thing
always of this thing.

It would not
move against anything
to know
to know it is moving.

Is this thing
is actually things
themselves are actually this
is therefore
how.

Lively enough
to be
a thing in
itself itself
moving
does not have to
move
anything to know
it does it does not
need that
it does not
need that there.

Then we have then
we have never be
repeating, never
be alive and it is alive
it is never saying
saying anything
never be the same.

How do you
like what
you have.

Asking I began
of any one.
Inside them
what they are.
One can make a portrait.

I wonder now
to stand still
alive
to be a new
way, success
of a way
with failure.

My she is sure.

Another thing
to think about
about anything.

The habit of conceiving
talking and listening
listening was
as was listening
so doing
the rhythm
of listening was
listening.

As I say
was doing
there were the little things
some
one resembling some
one
any one
can.

Any one can notice this
thing
notice this
resemblance
and this is a different thing.

In other words
of any one
as they are,
as they are.

As they are.

3. MELANCTHA IMAGE

Warm broad glow
to negro sunshine
the child loves *all* the smoke!—
men, and the engines,
and a kind of being.

Steady soothing world
in motion in a moving van dream
need not work in it or own it
—*child watching*
 through a hole in the fence!

Loves *all* the noise
of the pounding,
the pounding down, elbow
up and piston.

4. If You Had Two Husbands

If you had two husbands.
If you had two husbands.
Well, not exactly.
If you had two husbands would you be willing to take everything and be satisfied to live in a large house with love and a view and plenty of flowers and friends at table and the young ones and cousins who said nothing.
This is what happened.

She expressed everything.
She is worthy of signing a will.
And mentioning what she wished.
She was brought up by her mother or her father. She had meaning and she was careful in reading. She read marvelously. She moved.
She was pleased. She was thirty-four. She was flavored by reason of much memory and recollection.

Foreword.

I cannot believe it.
I cannot realize it.
I cannot see it.
It is what happened.
First there was wonder.
Really wonder.

Wonder by means of what.
Wonder by means of measure.
Measuring what.
Heights.
How high.
A little, but very.
This was not all.
There were wonderful spots such as were seen by a queen. This came to be a system and hers. Really it was a treasure. And mine.

In their beginning was delight. Not signing papers or anything though papers were signed. It was a choice.
I ramble when I mention it.
I remember something.
When did I settle that.
Yesterday.

Early life.

They were not miserably young. They were older than another. She was gliding. It is by nearly weekly learning that it comes to be exact. It never was in dispute.
They were gayly and not gorgeous. They were not gorgeous at all. They were obliging. They were never almost never another.

Early days of shading.

Make a single piece of sun and make a violet bloom. Early days of swimming and stroke and sun on time and makes for shine and warms the day and sun and not to stay and not to stay away. Not to stay in. Out from the whole wide world he chose her. And that is what is said.

No opposition.

If you had a little likeness and hoped for more terror. If you had a refusal and were slender. If you had cuffs and jackets and astonishing kinds of fever would you stop talking. Would I. Would you not consider it necessary to talk over affairs. Would we.

It was chance that never made them miss it. They did not miss it because it was there. They did not mean to be particular. They were not aching. It was noiseless and they were clever. Who was clever. The way they had of seeing each other.

They were caressing.

They had sound sense.

They were questioned.

They had likeness. Likeness to what. Likeness to loving. Who had likeness to loving. They had likeness to loving. They had a likeness to loving because they did not measure.

They were fixed by that, not licensed. They were seen,

not treasured. They were pronounced, not restless. They were reasoning, not progressing. I do not wish to imply that there was any remedy.

I cannot state that anyone was disappointed. I cannot state that any one was ever disappointed by willingly heaping confusion in small places. No confusion is reasonable. Anybody can be nervous.

This is wishing.

Listing.

She cannot exercise obligation.
Cannot believe cheating.
Cannot shut my heart.
Cannot cherish.
Cannot deceive.
Cannot see between.
Between what and most.
I cannot answer either.
This is not advice.

I am not telling the story I am repeating what I have been reading.

Length of time or times.

She agreed. She said I would have known by this time. Or should. I don't like to think about it. It would have led to so much. There is could. Not that I am disappointed. I know all that I am to happiness and it is to be happy and I am happy. I am so completely happy that I mention it.

In writing now I find it more of a strain because now I write by sentences. I don't mean that I feel it here. I feel it here and by this time I do mention it. I do not feel the significance of this list.

So.

If you had two husbands I don't mean that as a guess or a wish. I believe in what I saw and what I see. I believe finally in what I see, in where I satisfy my extreme shadow.

Not a beginning.

Let me describe the white room. A white room isn't cold or warm. A white room is not meant to be icy. A white room is worthy of articles.

He pleased she pleased everybody. He pleased her.

This kills.

She was attracted by the time. I did not know there were clocks.

All this was after it was not necessary for us to be there all the time. That was clear. Who we were. We often were enlightening. We were light. By way of what. By way of steps or doors. Ways out.

I remember very well the day she asked me if I were patient. Of course I was. I was patient enough, of course I was patient enough.

It isn't easy to be restless.

If sitting is not developed.

If standing is not open.

If active action is represented by lying and if tears are beside delight, it is a rope.

Pleasant days.

So to speak.
Sand today.
Saturday.
Sunday.
I pray.
For what.
Laugh.
I know it.
You do.
Let us go then.
One must be willing.
One is.
I was not disappointed.

Pleasant days brother. I don't mean this thing. I don't mean calling aloud though I called aloud. Glittering streets. I was splendid and sorrowful. I could catch my breath.

I do not see much necessity for believing that it would have occurred as it did occur if sun and September and the hope had not been mentioned. Why not be determined. Why not oppose. Why not settle on flowers, speak cryingly, loath to detain her, or to free. How does anyone speak.

I am not satisfied.

Their end.

Anyone can help weeping.
By wise by wisdom.
I am indifferent am I.
Not a bite.
Call me handsome.
It was a nice fate.
Any one would see.
Why not have politeness.

I have utter confusion.
No two can be alike.
They are and they are not stubborn.
Some are.

Please me.
I was mistaken.
Anyways.
By that.

Do not refuse to be wild.
Do not refuse to be all.
We have decided not to withstand it.
We would rather not have the home.

I am going to continue humming.

Suite: Mac Low

1. AUXILIARIES

Should has older urges let down,
has aspects soured.
Older letters die, even reasons.
Urges revel; grace even should
let even terms
down over waning needs.

Could of used less drama
of fanfare.
Used self's especial drama
less ego (self, self).
Drama reaches always (my always).

Would oval under lofty deal.
Oval value after loss.
Under nothing, deal even real.
Lofty oval, free two years.
Deal even after loss.

2. Dannemora (for Mac Low)

Word over reason dream
over version eager reason
reason eager after stable over need
dream reason eager after mean.

Over version eager reason
version eager reason stable idiom over need
eager after gesture eager reason
reason eager after stable over need.

Reason eager after stable over need
eager after gesture eager reason
after facet telling eager reason
stable telling after basic lesson eager
over version eager reason
need eager eager dream.

Dream reason eager after mean
reason eager after stable over need
eager after gesture eager reason
after facet telling eager reason
mean eager after need.

Over version eager reason
version eager reason stable idiom over need
eager after gesture eager reason
reason eager after stable over need.

Version eager reason stable idiom over need
eager after gesture eager reason
reason eager after stable over need
stable telling after basic lesson eager
idiom dream idiom over mean.
Over version eager reason
need eager eager dream.

Eager after gesture eager reason
after facet telling eager reason
gesture eager stable telling urges reason eager
eager after eager reason
reason eager after stable over need.

Reason eager after stable over need
eager after gesture eager reason
after facet telling eager reason
stable telling after basic lesson eager
over version eager reason
need eager eager dream.

Reason eager after stable over need
eager after gesture eager reason
after facet telling eager reason
stable telling after basic lesson eager
over version eager reason
need eager eager dream.

Eager after gesture eager reason
after facet telling eager reason
gesture eager stable telling urges reason eager
eager after gesture eager reason
reason eager after stable over need.

After facet telling eager reason
facet after core eager telling
telling eager lesson lesson idiom need gesture
eager after gesture eager reason
reason eager after stable over need.

Stable telling after basic lesson eager
telling eager lesson lesson idiom need dream
after facet telling eager reason
basic after stable idiom core
lesson eager stable stable over need
eager after gesture eager reason.

Over version eager reason
version eager reason stable idiom over need
eager after gesture eager reason
reason eager after stable over need.

Need eager eager dream
eager after gesture eager reason
eager after gesture eager reason
dream reason eager after mean.

4

Dream reason eager after mean
reason eager after stable over need
eager after gesture eager reason
after facet telling eager reason
mean eager after need.

Reason eager after stable over need
eager after gesture eager reason
after facet telling eager reason
stable telling after basic lesson eager
over version eager reason
need eager eager dream.

Eager after gesture eager reason
after facet telling eager reason
gesture eager stable telling urges reason eager
eager after gesture eager reason
reason eager after stable over need.

After facet telling eager reason
facet after core eager telling
telling eager lesson lesson idiom need gesture
eager after gesture eager reason
reason eager after stable over need.

Mean eager after need
eager after gesture eager reason
after facet telling eager reason
need eager eager dream.

5

Over version eager reason
version eager reason stable idiom over need
eager after gesture eager reason
reason eager after stable over need.

Version eager reason stable idiom over need
eager after gesture eager reason
reason eager after stable over need
stable telling after basic lesson eager

idiom dream idiom over mean
over version eager reason
need eager eager dream.

Eager after gesture eager reason
after facet telling eager reason
gesture eager stable telling urges reason eager
eager after gesture eager reason
reason eager after stable over need.

Reason eager after stable over need
eager after gesture eager reason
after facet telling eager reason
stable telling after basic lesson eager
over version eager reason
need eager eager dream.

6

Version eager reason stable idiom over need
eager after gesture eager reason
reason eager after stable over need
stable telling after basic lesson eager
idiom dream idiom over mean
over version eager reason
need eager eager dream.

Eager after gesture eager reason
after facet telling eager reason
gesture eager stable telling urges reason eager
eager after gesture eager reason
reason eager after stable over need.

Reason eager after stable over need
eager after gesture eager reason
after facet telling eager reason
stable telling after basic lesson eager
over version eager reason
need eager eager dream.

Stable telling after basic lesson eager
telling eager lesson lesson idiom need gesture
after facet telling eager reason
basic after stable idiom core
lesson eager stable stable over need
eager after gesture eager reason.

Idiom dream idiom over mean
dream reason eager after mean
idiom dream idiom over mean
over version eager reason
mean eager after need.

Over version eager reason
version eager reason stable idiom over need
eager after gesture eager reason
reason eager after stable over need.

Need eager eager dream
eager after gesture eager reason
eager after gesture eager reason
dream reason eager after mean.

7

Eager after gesture eager reason
after facet telling eager reason
gesture eager stable telling urges reason eager
eager after gesture eager reason
reason eager after stable over need.

After facet telling eager reason
facet after core eager telling
telling eager lesson lesson idiom need gesture
eager after gesture eager reason
reason eager after stable over need.

Gesture eager stable telling urges reason eager
eager after gesture eager reason
stable telling after basic lesson eager
telling eager lesson lesson idiom need gesture
urges reason gesture eager stable
reason eager after stable over need
eager after gesture eager reason.

Eager after gesture eager reason
after facet telling eager reason
gesture eager stable telling urges reason eager
eager after gesture eager reason
reason eager after stable over need.

Reason eager after stable over need
eager after gesture eager reason
after facet telling eager reason
stable telling after basic lesson eager
over version eager reason
need eager eager dream.

8

Reason eager after stable over need
eager after gesture eager reason
after facet telling eager reason
stable telling after basic lesson eager
over version eager reason
need eager eager dream.

Eager after gesture eager reason
after facet telling eager reason
gesture eager stable telling urges reason eager
eager after gesture eager reason
reason eager after stable over need.

After facet telling eager reason
facet after core eager telling
telling eager lesson lesson idiom need gesture
eager after gesture eager reason
reason eager after stable over need.

Stable telling after basic lesson eager
telling eager lesson lesson idiom need dream
after facet telling eager reason
basic after stable idiom core
lesson eager stable stable over need
eager after gesture eager reason.

Over version eager reason
version eager reason stable idiom over need
eager after gesture eager reason
reason eager after stable over need.

Need eager eager dream
eager after gesture eager reason
eager after gesture eager reason
dream reason eager after mean.

9

Reason eager after stable over need
eager after gesture eager reason
after facet telling eager reason

stable telling after basic lesson eager
over version eager reason
need eager eager dream.

Eager after gesture eager reason
after facet telling eager reason
gesture eager stable telling urges reason eager
eager after gesture eager reason
reason eager after stable over need.

After facet telling eager reason
facet after core eager telling
telling eager lesson lesson idiom need gesture
eager after gesture eager reason
reason eager after stable over need.

Stable telling after basic lesson eager
telling eager lesson lesson idiom need dream
after facet telling eager reason
basic after stable idiom core
lesson eager stable stable over need
eager after gesture eager reason.

Over version eager reason
version eager reason stable idiom over need
eager after gesture eager reason
reason eager after stable over need.

Need eager eager dream
eager after gesture eager reason
eager after gesture eager reason
dream reason eager after mean.

10

Eager after gesture eager reason
after facet telling eager reason
gesture eager stable telling urges reason eager
eager after gesture eager reason
reason eager after stable over need.

After facet telling eager reason
facet after core eager telling
telling eager lesson lesson idiom need gesture
eager after gesture eager reason
reason eager after stable over need.

Gesture eager stable telling urges reason eager
eager after gesture eager reason
stable telling after basic lesson eager
telling eager lesson lesson idiom need gesture
urges reason gesture eager stable
reason eager after stable over need
eager after gesture eager reason.

Eager after gesture eager reason
after facet telling eager reason
gesture eager stable telling urges reason eager
eager after gesture eager reason
reason eager after stable over need.

Reason eager after stable over need
eager after gesture eager reason
after facet telling eager reason
stable telling after basic lesson eager
over version eager reason
need eager eager dream.

II

After facet telling eager reason
facet after core eager telling
telling eager lesson lesson idiom need gesture
eager after gesture eager reason
reason eager after stable over need.

Facet after core eager telling
after facet telling eager reason
core over reason eager
eager after gesture eager reason
telling eager lesson lesson idiom need gesture.

Telling eager lesson lesson idiom need gesture
eager after gesture eager reason
lesson eager stable stable over need
lesson eager stable stable over need
idiom dream idiom over mean
need eager eager dream
gesture eager stable telling urges reason eager.

Eager after gesture eager reason
after facet telling eager reason
gesture eager stable telling urges reason eager
eager after gesture eager reason
reason eager after stable over need.

Reason eager after stable over need
eager after gesture eager reason
after facet telling eager reason
stable telling after basic lesson eager
over version eager reason
reason eager after stable over need.

12

Stable telling after basic lesson eager
telling eager lesson lesson idiom need gesture
after facet telling eager reason
basic after stable idiom core
lesson eager stable stable over need
eager after gesture eager reason.

Telling eager lesson lesson idiom need gesture
eager after gesture eager reason
lesson eager stable stable over need
lesson eager stable stable over need
idiom dream idiom over mean
need eager eager dream
gesture eager stable telling urges reason eager.

After facet telling eager reason
facet after core eager telling
telling eager lesson lesson idiom need gesture
eager after gesture eager reason
reason eager after stable over need.

Basic after stable idiom core
after facet telling eager reason
stable telling after basic lesson eager
idiom dream idiom over mean
core over reason eager.

Lesson eager stable stable over need
eager after gesture eager reason
stable telling after basic lesson eager
stable telling after basic lesson eager
over version eager reason
need eager eager dream.

Eager after gesture eager reason
after facet telling eager reason
gesture eager stable telling urges reason eager
eager after gesture eager reason
reason eager after stable over need.

Over version eager reason
version eager reason stable idiom over need
eager after gesture eager reason
reason eager after stable over need.

Version eager reason stable idiom over need
eager after gesture eager reason
reason eager after stable over need
stable telling after basic lesson eager
idiom dream idiom over mean
over version eager reason
need eager eager dream.

Eager after gesture eager reason
after facet telling eager reason
gesture eager stable telling urges reason eager
eager after gesture eager reason
reason eager after stable over need.

Reason eager after stable over need
eager after gesture eager reason
after facet telling eager reason
stable telling after basic lesson eager
over version eager reason
need eager eager dream.

14

Need eager eager dream
eager after gesture eager reason
eager after gesture eager reason
dream reason eager after mean.

Eager after gesture eager reason
after facet telling eager reason
gesture eager stable telling urges reason eager
eager after gesture eager reason
reason eager after stable over need.

Eager after gesture eager reason
after facet telling eager reason
gesture eager stable telling urges reason eager
eager after gesture eager reason
reason eager after stable over need.

Dream reason eager after mean
reason eager after stable over need
eager after gesture eager reason
after facet telling eager reason
mean eager after need.

15

Dream reason eager after mean
reason eager after stable over need
eager after gesture eager reason
after facet telling eager reason
mean eager after need.

Reason eager after stable over need
eager after gesture eager reason
after facet telling eager reason
stable telling after basic lesson eager
over version eager reason
need eager eager dream.

Eager after gesture eager reason
after facet telling eager reason
gesture eager stable telling urges reason eager
eager after gesture eager reason
reason eager after stable over need.

After facet telling eager reason
facet after core eager telling
telling eager lesson lesson idiom need gesture
eager after gesture eager reason
reason eager after stable over need.

Mean eager after need
eager after gesture eager reason
after facet telling eager reason
need eager eager dream.

16

Reason eager after stable over need
eager after gesture eager reason
after facet telling eager reason
stable telling after basic lesson eager
over version eager reason
need eager eager dream.

Eager after gesture eager reason
after facet telling eager reason
gesture eager stable telling urges reason eager
eager after gesture eager reason
reason eager after stable over need.

After facet telling eager reason
facet after core eager telling
telling eager lesson lesson idiom need gesture
eager after gesture eager reason
reason eager after stable over need.

Stable telling after basic lesson eager
telling eager lesson lesson idiom need dream
after facet telling eager reason
basic after stable idiom core
lesson eager stable stable over need
eager after gesture eager reason.

Over version eager reason
version eager reason stable idiom over need
eager after gesture eager reason
reason eager after stable over need.

Need eager eager dream
eager after gesture eager reason
eager after gesture eager reason
dream reason eager after mean.

17

Eager after gesture eager reason
after facet telling eager reason
gesture eager stable telling urges reason eager
eager after gesture eager reason
reason eager after stable over need.

After facet telling eager reason
facet after core eager telling
telling eager lesson lesson idiom need gesture
eager after gesture eager reason
reason eager after stable over need.

Gesture eager stable telling urges reason eager
eager after gesture eager reason
stable telling after basic lesson eager
telling eager lesson lesson idiom need gesture
urges reason gesture eager stable
reason eager after stable over need
eager after gesture eager reason.

Eager after gesture eager reason
after facet telling eager reason
gesture eager stable telling urges reason eager
eager after gesture eager reason
reason eager after stable over need.

Reason eager after stable over need
eager after gesture eager reason
after facet telling eager reason
stable telling after basic lesson eager
over version eager reason
need eager eager dream.

After facet telling eager reason
facet after core eager telling
telling eager lesson lesson idiom need gesture
eager after gesture eager reason
reason eager after stable over need.

Facet after core eager telling
after facet telling eager reason
core over reason eager
eager after gesture eager reason
telling eager lesson lesson idiom need gesture.

Telling eager lesson lesson idiom need gesture
eager after gesture eager reason
lesson eager stable stable over need
lesson eager stable stable over need
idiom dream idiom over mean
need eager eager dream
gesture eager stable telling urges reason eager.

Eager after gesture eager reason
after facet telling eager reason
gesture eager stable telling urges reason eager
eager after gesture eager reason
reason eager after stable over need.

Reason eager after stable over need
eager after gesture eager reason
after facet telling eager reason
stable telling after basic lesson eager
over version eager reason
reason eager after stable over need.

19

Mean eager after need
eager after gesture eager reason
after facet telling eager reason
need eager eager dream.

Eager after gesture eager reason
after facet telling eager reason
gesture eager stable telling urges reason eager
eager after gesture eager reason
reason eager after stable over need.

After facet telling eager reason
facet after core eager telling
telling eager lesson lesson idiom need gesture
eager after gesture eager reason
reason eager after stable over need.

Need eager eager dream
eager after gesture eager reason
eager after gesture eager reason
dream reason eager after mean.

20

And so on . . .

3. A BIT WRONG BUT NOT AT ALL DEAD WRONG

(being a syllabic replica of Jackson Mac Low's "A Lack of Balance but Not Fatal")

Erosion mated in oceans
imploring of a floor.
Chortles of wreckage in torsion.

Enable the sifting. A last lens
in eyes able of. Indecent
in inches out to sound an alarm aloud
lest one were wished. Anyway, wailing's wrong.

Intention above a sign.
Not the essence of a narrative.

The head missed by only feet.
Tends to others and not to a horse.
Hesitant homes in a fantasy
of a full-fated omen bearing rain:
end of a chapter. A balk is what a shout is.

The dark political mess. Looseness lectured us:
uneven words. Belittle youth for pay.
Heed the force a minute and amphibians play.
Lit one pocket up, a litmus, no variance.
Intuition leaning east for awhile.
A low-lying amount, sea-swell
in an ocean weather with a vertebrate, easing task.

A frame is hung. A bed-manned phone.
Barmbrack cools on a board. Tongues roll.
A rarer wattle gave us two for halving.
Too fast for pride plus an overture.
Lend to scribe the spent account. Teacher reach
reaches of an aspect. Or two of things.

Efface indecision well. Re-seed a cloud.

Off-shore fins good luck. The old equation.
Jerusalem. Impieties abound,
reveal an error. A case of finger lengths

shut up in a boxcar, in a broke side show
of lye in the eyes. Ring mastery. The heave
under fire. The best ingot unshaken
is of the shifted is the gist of ancient porches.
Heresies in senses breeding apathies.

Hence the bonfires sear a new scent, a rise.
Not yet known for knowing inconsistently.
Chance this innocence above a bad fascist.
A depth belies a stencil's touch. A recusant
bore a bin of corn liquor. Fetish is.
Ashen cast was evident. Invention.
Murmansk a thousand leagues of low wages. Forms
formed. A dulling portable feeds a queen.
The king's creatures heft intoxication about
athwart a base sentence to fall. Real rings off.

Sword is changing divine old game it berated.
All winter cold for feeling. No drinks tried.
Avid thrashings. A wry sense killed. Seeds
for straw returned. English in principle,
sometimes sporting morals of a pest: so.
Cost her war's inevitable fee,   *belle chic*
to propound. Crenelation is replete.
Eating best able after vespers. Supposing
the taint returned. Some future tested. Optical
tints in a twist. A fiercely achromatic
readout was hid. Fleetness triumphed. A shade
fades in and out unfurling a shadow. The law on loan.

No less, a bread famine. Withholding air.
Clothes of a bureaucrat sure to surface in winter.
The last to doubt, order out east to a station going slow.
Forever free aboard and denuded. A chest.
Tunnelling. A piece of a key in a moon phase
or might be. Phone markets off and vermin.
What was is the is of delusion to the mocking, sir,
a late fine brought. Or not. Sow deeper.
Wounds festered on the devlish physiognomy. Art of us messed.

Tricks and stones thrown. Pursue the thin things.
Took some of sources in bitter strife. Catch is
catch the alabaster, heads in the grate. Dues.
Event of theme bans hunger. Search to injure urges.
Covet is a doubt of aging, bad as the bells.
As future. A too grim light is canned. No wonder.
Frozen past dooms this laugh, this sensation
of a jest. No not ever the action openly
away. Balled up for a year or years the rusting water
of a gun weapon to violate or turn a head thing
to a dream. Scenes in lots incomplete. No dream.

Javajazyk

Javajazyk

(A linguistic romance ending in prayer)

os

Vasteny garsled Ombaly, tahk unda febala. Cune Ombali, Vasteny adwarl. Quersten formaladhin, Vasteny lorkaleet deveen.

Trongar sebber destel. Quechebar pourtch ak tikavoorn, iodar ras. Las ludanay labloonder fum. Vasteny, Ombaly, garstule.

Fecher fas Ombaly. Ombaly garsolde Vast'. Een ravaor ras, razz jidder, fon Ombaly. Jasser dhe: unda dheo jasser. Unda cubalo Ombale.

Ombaly susOmbaly! Ke sha va. Os en os enosenos duva. Farus osh din proke.

Vasty lasch duver.

Vasty yashin.

Viv Vasty, sudVasteny, clondriquin tuelle.

Horish ashey.

ba

Ketcher vissal, clam destin dus vip Ombaly. Dheo sussness, ol pester. Dheo kirchin mas, ik feestor. Ombaly tremp tentergin unda feen. Dheo rais, tahk munas flor, betroll defentieder dra dhe't. Nofloe linchwa dheo vasty.

Horbis. Actash horbi. Vasteny mawlin flagron toon sliviast en saschid prustor. Nav alixin sodor rin, dhe juk. Dhe fayon:

"Ombaly, susOmbaly! Boyon fintay sool: gobber?"

Vasteny haberd. Dhe floen. SusOmbaly rigin turkle doan turkelan. Borsd en borsul. Fremd en fraul, deb senesalt gena marmuan. Aben sobul fanstra gjon.

cha

Ain astelay dheoth oberone: os, ba, cha, tow, chena, din, bos, boba, bacha, bato, bachen, bin, chos, chiba, acha, chata, chachen, chin, tos, toba, tucha, atow, tachen, tin, cheso, cheba, chencha, cheto, achena, chindin, dinos, diba, dicha, ditow, ditchen, adin, enos, enos enosenos.

Ombalyda ba sanda, bas aig, bas eener, bas awnu'daun, bas elda; dh'os nit, os ot, os elma.

Vastenyda ba sanda, bas aig, bas eener, bas awnu'daun, bas elda' dh'os nit, os ot, os elc, pudda bas orz.

OmbaVastenyda tow sanda, tows aig, tows eener, tows awnu'daun, tows elda; dhet ba nit, bas ot, achul os elma unda os elc. A bas orz.

Ombalyina es du: chouper, furder, woder, cowoder, schless—Ombaly enfurtela.

Vastenyina es due: chouper, furder, woder, cowoder, schless—Vasteny enfurtela.

Vasteny garseld Ombaly en enfurtelan. Dhe chencha; dheo chindin.

tow

Dheo ot Bashenin. Bashenin actur fontel ne rubumpa. Rubumpa achen susrubumpa ogen bayen. Chelust veder farol sed adair nin gento fim, parken den molow. Vasteny un Ombaly chak Bashenin.

Avta adin: sodan flageltint, ocorsetrown tempro jene. Anin neesra febeset, cra fash oc fashenjik.

Avta bacha: maudin peckreltcha iz, ne clantis debengronchi, prolem.

Avta chin: os en os enosenos.

Aftadal uk Bashenoca urba donason. Depews relaun dober maun duvert. Krebble teeha flal craben hune vork. En Bashenin grovly vasefrul, vasedron, chopare.

Fossle sunlin jenda min. Elfastid illiol nagh, veron quido pash avul. Rimdra praetly kash robeldun Bashenoca.

Trantabul abenard, ducile litmum tenker. Astravalejen okvaldus fut, nenner rill fodelle. Jendra unda ogelish meack munder lobel drahs octibillil jok; fremdrul zay chel gastin acker ho. Hashbiligum fuertan gow bren enstominast enjul. En Bashenin muern chabble, muern flant, awfor filliol obdel ghone.

Zutmagul eep, eep pin foln. Drerais cuvern relequer. Cebedec ik bedekay frolm fudder mumm. Jewble …

Voboder noclost furngila dair fumbalen dik. Rovonos lomante queth, nodder drentch hemersteln isk fundor. Claust flal dembrel, tercenembren gindra clanch. Abduciak abdeen.

Poncha duncherest nock, fibin traisto abeno. Aliquonda jimes feen, castar ankfuden douber. Cavalaskteky dimen listry ninck ot quobell vester gohnort ort. Dek debantry frelden klongow gowl. Ebterfile fainder int endert lebowl nock obtid un jangrestule tiffer. Meshlew fondintine ut norble runder. Haspal lounden indegh drinton tokle clendras. A naus senachtervol, florus tankle derstune jahb. Felsprut dungren jast.

chena

Vasteny chak: Tas van yevant na stavetas yesa. Tyvas stest anteyva yeva. Ensas nysanta senya, avast yenty neast eva sta. Nysva nesva teena, ty na avsa svay. Teas tsaveny tyn.

Ombaly chak: Mabo lymb ol alyoun blamb. Bally mool, bally ombal yoom, alayon abala yomalo. Bol yob yb yomb, mobal labymoba. Balom labal mombal yalla. Blo yallo yoy yalla, yalla, yalla yomyalla ym yall. Bym bal yoom, yoob!

Vasteny chak (a pelo): Taspelo pelovan yevant napelo napelo stavetas, peloyesa. Tyvaspelo, avastapelo peloyenty. Ensasepelo nysanta enyapelo, avastepelo peloyenty neast evapelo pelospapelo. Nysvapelo nesva, teenapelo pelona avasapelo. Peloteas tsavasnopelo tyn.

Ombaly chak (a pelo): Pelomabo lymb ol pelo alyoumpelo blamb. Bally pelomool, ballypelo yoom, alayompelo pelobola yamabo. Pelobeol yobopelo yb yombopelo, mobal labymobopelo. Pelobalom pelolabol mombal peloyalla. Blopelo yallo peloym yallapeolo, yallapelo ympelo yallopelo ym yallopelo. Pelobym, pelobal, yoompelo, loyoob.

OmbaVasty chak (debunchuntian): Be deb ded eb beed, beded. Debun nube dun, debun. Echen unch bedee dun bu. Ditun det bun chit dunchen, tichen dinch. Ande nat ched nuntch thid shundu ubchin nuu.

din

Selugnin opalast deweur musch coonder oshen. Cune abtehan razza nos geen. Debula frip Ombaly unda Vasteny sheel, dash hever duvill neckaan. Of'deliort drenshul trastel evenby, sare. Belew bewaner, kastelan forbur. Eger esheal cleevor. Tib sut jenkor foodly mim. Eth nawhrla congere bule.

Ovdelaz ninaselk, touvre jil muvee. Gondra hoblen hoblen dil, Wngra jucha tooster, tegn estip. Wargel evtoplaza, mayi absun ornfel tow. Chibber ninch gerhen plinna, javajazyk.

bos

Akmal desheener vasin, jerezun fader. Glassingla frare bedit luben rosma, neg nulen. Limmit sen gail fla'modder gezeur. Hespitch dlimnor dormle lush fone der, evdemia ic. Moggle mowstra gib; ter shink hutcha vahs gle dhenan, yo Vasty.

Vasteny jerden forq. Dhe mawlin livvent krasp mattor monda gink. Lofleeden unda freen, jeremano dool. Prostone rotir montaux lant dimter nissel nane. Halmest ankra flamz loovett pol. Tavseterole deegon wohler. Clair juzet mawnker massa. Betuden jizzer clae hawt vuzere. Menonka, menune; fla legunin chint, fobelok susOmbaly. Camber mawn, fichter drapo'nunk es bundra phool. Hopter inchoven dewse, blondher.

Chas jinder mornd, jamunder. Handen gashela dubare. Bluston neffer ant ghabeshalew, horc nastrode farus un ninta. Abinchaver mus, musso mus mussomus. Muso cle, musso mus. Jinmussup musso mus musso. E musso demus musso musso musso temusto muss. Emus musso musso men. Demos mosso mosso muss; gerusummos geru. Musto musso muss. Amasto mass emasso mass. Demass dehaldemass, clemuss umass. Mass mass factomasso fancter.

eeeeeeeeeeeeeeeeeeeeeeeeeeeeeeeeeeeeeeeeeeeAkmu bedit

climnor desheener evdemia fader. Glassingla hespitch ic jerezun krasp, luben moggle neg onkra. Prostone forq rotir shink ter unda vasin wohler montaux Vasty ebenfidzy.

ooooooooooooooooooooooooooooooooooooooooooooo-nevercherlanka slenluss trull, naper dewant lesure. Sush aventaben in durure campeu sumtussure feen. Abashen oonda ossen. Archest eener debree. Shellus ostily dran, fasso lebber. Denchwan vornus oan. Claslip misstrul tabroodrune. Fastion gidder drap.

aaaaaaaaaaaaaaaaaaaaaaaaaaaaaaaaaaaaaaaaanifallon twarl. Kikostor fint iiiiiiiiiiiiiiiiiiiiiiiiiiiisayul. Dewser davull provole seraspid nol, ab centary. Foggle un opfule.

uuuuuuuuuuuuuuuuuuuuuuuuuuuuuuuuuuuuuuuuuuwu-wuwuwuwuwnobano

banobanobanobanobanobanobanovaduba a frentch amba.

"Ombaly! Ombaly! SusOmbaly!"

boba

Clero te veret. Clero te vere. Clero te veret. Clero te ver. Clero te veret. Claro teve. Clero te veret. Clero tev. Clero te veret. Clerot e. Clerto te veret. Clero. Clero te veret. Cler. Clero te veret. Cle. Clero te veret. Clickaclickaclickaclickaclick.

Dmose vo wosov. Dmose vo woso. Dmose vo wosov. Dmose vo wos. Dmose vo wosov. Dmose vo wo. Dmose vo wosov. Dmose vow. Dmose vo wosov. Dmosevo. Dmose vo wosov. Dmosev. Dmose vo wosov. Dmose. Dmose vo wosov. Dmos. Dmose vo wosov. Dmo. D'meodemodemodemodemawdemoodema.

Fneto we xetew. Fneto wexete. Fneto we xetew. Fneto wexet. Fneto we xetew. Fnetowexe. Fneto we xetew. Fnetowex. Fneto we xetew. Fnetowe. Fneto we xetew. Fneto. Fneto we xetew. Fnet. Fneto we xetew. Fnaffanaffanaffanaffanew, dul, boahn; ta, pluh, upch.

bacha

Az za, za zaz. Za zaza a za. Aza, zaza. Aza aza, az. Bazy ay. Bay zazy azy baz. Zab zazy, za zay. Baz a bazzy. Ba zay. Cabazy azy bay. Bazaz azbac, yaxca yaxa yaz. Bayab cayab yb. Azy zab cabay. Cydax dawyz zaba waxa yaca wayz. Bawa zay, dacaw caday zaw. Yavex wava. Veada cayz. Za bax da bawyz dab. Zavad ya, yawax zew. Vug abaz duva wa, fabda weyfuvva. Zefa cade ub yav uce. Fedayac waffew zev. Taga ba guvyut bude, cabaw yetzega fatug. Zutafaged tuger, fugad vega yafa gub, wedd. Tyz ba vyzta dgget; xaba fedda dutuwyz, guff. Vashud zuhz. Habad fuvwas steegeb huz. Vustude cuva. Yadefeghust debefust su. Dibaver vavas raw, didigger uvess ror. Havtit zachusa gayz, ighel, ribadrist, debaw quan. Daba whans juntul quabat waxal juve. Yarsta fegh tudess wazatch. Wop ordas stubba krure. Jipkaddur deburk tastas gabba, yaz. Troge kabba dees, ustus gefa gafa, olgasru. Zalda pro twellus qu zazawas. Lidor tab tul crowfult gek. Monus uzer arben clowder shap. Neandra jindra, acton oberle flufta dit. Klemeno clont alfustor dresta hinger mastun floder, mar amanall.

bato

O theca theca theca theca
O theca theca theca theca theca
O theca theca theca theca
O theca theca theca theca

O theca shenga shenga theca
O theca shenga shenga theca
O theca shenga shenga shenga
O theca theca koom

O theca theca koom theca
O theca theca koom theca theca
O theca koom theca theca
O theca koom

Koom koom koom shenga shenga
Koom koom koom shenga shenga
O koom shenga shenga koom shenga
Shenga koom shenga shenga shenga shenga

Shenga shenga koom shenga shenga
Koom koom shenga shenga shenga
Koom koom shenga shenga shenga
O shenga koom

Shenga shenga koom shenga shenga
Koom koom shenga shenga shenga
Koom koom shenga shenga shenga
Shenga koom shenga shenga shenga
O shenga koom koom theca theca.

NEW AMERICAN POETRY SERIES (NAP)

31. *Polyverse*, Lee Ann Brown
[WINNER NEW AMERICAN POETRY SERIES COMPETITION 1995]
32. *Response*, Juliana Spahr
[WINNER NATIONAL POETRY SERIES 1995]

For a complete list of our poetry publications
write us at Sun & Moon Press
6026 Wilshire Boulevard
Los Angeles, California 90036